The Successes of Socialism

A Complete Chronicle of the Successes of Socialism Throughout History

Joshua P. Perry

The Successes of Socialism

Copyright © 2018 Joshua P. Perry

All rights reserved.

DEDICATION

This book is dedicated to the millions of victims of the failed experiment that is socialism throughout human history.

The Successes of Socialism

The Successes of Socialism

CONTENTS

Acknowledgments	i
Chapter One	Pg 2
Chapter Two	Pg 28
Chapter Three	Pg 52
Chapter Four	Pg 66
Chapter Five	Pg 99
Chapter Six	Pg 137
Chapter Seven	Pg 141
Chapter Eight	Pg 188
Chapter Nine	Pg 201
Chapter Ten	Pg 222

The Successes of Socialism

ACKNOWLEDGMENTS

For better or for worse, I'd like to acknowledge anyone and everyone on Twitter who -- depending on whom is being asked -- drove me to genius or insanity.

Also, to the love of my life, Sarah Quinlan.

The Successes of Socialism

The Successes of Socialism

The Successes of Socialism

The Successes of Socialism

The Successes of Socialism

The Successes of Socialism

The Successes of Socialism

The Successes of Socialism

The Successes of Socialism

The Successes of Socialism

The Successes of Socialism

The Successes of Socialism

The Successes of Socialism

The Successes of Socialism

The Successes of Socialism

The Successes of Socialism

The Successes of Socialism

The Successes of Socialism

The Successes of Socialism

The Successes of Socialism

The Successes of Socialism

The Successes of Socialism

The Successes of Socialism

The Successes of Socialism

The Successes of Socialism

The Successes of Socialism

The Successes of Socialism

The Successes of Socialism

The Successes of Socialism

The Successes of Socialism

The Successes of Socialism

The Successes of Socialism

The Successes of Socialism

The Successes of Socialism

The Successes of Socialism

The Successes of Socialism

The Successes of Socialism

The Successes of Socialism

The Successes of Socialism

The Successes of Socialism

The Successes of Socialism

The Successes of Socialism

The Successes of Socialism

The Successes of Socialism

The Successes of Socialism

The Successes of Socialism

The Successes of Socialism

The Successes of Socialism

The Successes of Socialism

The Successes of Socialism

The Successes of Socialism

The Successes of Socialism

The Successes of Socialism

The Successes of Socialism

The Successes of Socialism

The Successes of Socialism

The Successes of Socialism

The Successes of Socialism

The Successes of Socialism

The Successes of Socialism

The Successes of Socialism

The Successes of Socialism

The Successes of Socialism

The Successes of Socialism

The Successes of Socialism

The Successes of Socialism

The Successes of Socialism

The Successes of Socialism

The Successes of Socialism

The Successes of Socialism

The Successes of Socialism

The Successes of Socialism

The Successes of Socialism

The Successes of Socialism

The Successes of Socialism

The Successes of Socialism

The Successes of Socialism

The Successes of Socialism

The Successes of Socialism

The Successes of Socialism

The Successes of Socialism

The Successes of Socialism

The Successes of Socialism

The Successes of Socialism

The Successes of Socialism

The Successes of Socialism

The Successes of Socialism

The Successes of Socialism

The Successes of Socialism

The Successes of Socialism

The Successes of Socialism

The Successes of Socialism

The Successes of Socialism

The Successes of Socialism

The Successes of Socialism

The Successes of Socialism

The Successes of Socialism

The Successes of Socialism

The Successes of Socialism

The Successes of Socialism

The Successes of Socialism

The Successes of Socialism

The Successes of Socialism

The Successes of Socialism

The Successes of Socialism

The Successes of Socialism

The Successes of Socialism

The Successes of Socialism

The Successes of Socialism

The Successes of Socialism

The Successes of Socialism

The Successes of Socialism

The Successes of Socialism

The Successes of Socialism

The Successes of Socialism

The Successes of Socialism

The Successes of Socialism

The Successes of Socialism

The Successes of Socialism

The Successes of Socialism

The Successes of Socialism

The Successes of Socialism

The Successes of Socialism

The Successes of Socialism

The Successes of Socialism

The Successes of Socialism

The Successes of Socialism

The Successes of Socialism

The Successes of Socialism

The Successes of Socialism

The Successes of Socialism

The Successes of Socialism

The Successes of Socialism

The Successes of Socialism

The Successes of Socialism

The Successes of Socialism

The Successes of Socialism

The Successes of Socialism

The Successes of Socialism

The Successes of Socialism

The Successes of Socialism

The Successes of Socialism

The Successes of Socialism

The Successes of Socialism

The Successes of Socialism

The Successes of Socialism

The Successes of Socialism

The Successes of Socialism

The Successes of Socialism

The Successes of Socialism

The Successes of Socialism

The Successes of Socialism

The Successes of Socialism

The Successes of Socialism

The Successes of Socialism

The Successes of Socialism

The Successes of Socialism

The Successes of Socialism

The Successes of Socialism

The Successes of Socialism

The Successes of Socialism

The Successes of Socialism

The Successes of Socialism

The Successes of Socialism

The Successes of Socialism

The Successes of Socialism

The Successes of Socialism

The Successes of Socialism

The Successes of Socialism

The Successes of Socialism

The Successes of Socialism

The Successes of Socialism

The Successes of Socialism

The Successes of Socialism

The Successes of Socialism

The Successes of Socialism

The Successes of Socialism

The Successes of Socialism

The Successes of Socialism

The Successes of Socialism

The Successes of Socialism

The Successes of Socialism

The Successes of Socialism

The Successes of Socialism

The Successes of Socialism

The Successes of Socialism

The Successes of Socialism

The Successes of Socialism

The Successes of Socialism

The Successes of Socialism

The Successes of Socialism

The Successes of Socialism

The Successes of Socialism

The Successes of Socialism

The Successes of Socialism

The Successes of Socialism

The Successes of Socialism

The Successes of Socialism

The Successes of Socialism

The Successes of Socialism

The Successes of Socialism

The Successes of Socialism

The Successes of Socialism

The Successes of Socialism

The Successes of Socialism

The Successes of Socialism

The Successes of Socialism

The Successes of Socialism

The Successes of Socialism

The Successes of Socialism

The Successes of Socialism

The Successes of Socialism

The Successes of Socialism

The Successes of Socialism

The Successes of Socialism

The Successes of Socialism

The Successes of Socialism

The Successes of Socialism

The Successes of Socialism

The Successes of Socialism

The Successes of Socialism

The Successes of Socialism

The Successes of Socialism

The Successes of Socialism

The Successes of Socialism

The Successes of Socialism

The Successes of Socialism

The Successes of Socialism

The Successes of Socialism

ABOUT THE AUTHOR

Joshua P. Perry is a graduate of the University of Texas at Austin where he studied Government. Following his studies, he worked as an aide for U.S. Senator Ted Cruz in his U.S. Senate office in Washington, D.C. as well as for Sen. Cruz's presidential and senatorial campaigns.
Follow Josh on Twitter: @mrjoshperry.

www.ingramcontent.com/pod-product-compliance
Lightning Source LLC
Chambersburg PA
CBHW031616210526
45464CB00004B/1611